THE DARK FAMILY
SECRETS

DORIS CARTER

THIS IS A TRUE LIFE story about Doris Carter born in Barbados August 18, 1951.

I was born a twin, but my mother, Clara Carter, gave away my twin sister, Dorothy, at birth to Mrs. Allen of Tomberry Hill, Christ Church in Barbados. My mother was born in Panama, and my father was born in Barbados. I was raised by my grandmother, May Carter, until I was four years old, when my mother came to my grandmother's house one morning and took me on a bus to go with her. I was screaming and crying because I did not know my mother; the bus driver stopped the bus and kicked both of us off the bus. I ran to my grandmother's house and went under the bed because I was afraid of my mother.

When I was five years old, my sister, Johana, came to visit me. She told me she was going to take me to her house and then take me back to my grandmother. She took me to her house but never brought me back to my grandmother's house. I cried for days to go back to see my grandmother because I thought she was my mother.

At six years old, I went to see my grandmother. I was so happy to see her, I cried and asked her if I could stay with her for a few weeks.

While at my grandmother's house, I went to the beach with my cousins. While they were talking, I went into the beach where I almost drowned; the wave took me out, and I held on to my cousin's leg. They then rolled me to shore and tried to get the water out of my body. Since that day, they never took me back to the beach.

I went back to my mother's house and went to St. Mary's School then to St. Leonard's High School. My mother and father were separated. My mother had a boyfriend that didn't like me; he always came to the house to visit. One day, I told my father my mother had a boyfriend, and she was very mad at me because she didn't want my father to know she had a boyfriend. We then moved to Taylors Gap, Hindberry Road. There, my mother gave birth to identical twin girls. When the first girl came out, the midwife placed her in a basket on a table. I was staring at her because she looked pink. A few minutes later, the other baby girl came out, and the midwife cut her on the top lip. The baby started screaming. They always cut the second baby when they're born in my country so they were able to tell them apart. The midwife then put the baby in the basket and put the basket on her head and exited the room. I could hear my two sisters, Joyce and Johana, screaming and crying. I then begged my mother not to give them away. My sisters fell on the floor crying; my mother kept one of the twins and named her Esther.

We moved to Long Gap, Spooners Hill. My mother's boyfriend was married; his wife would stand at the bottom of the street and look. One day, she asked me if her husband was at my house, and I told her yes; he would stay, sometimes, for a few days.

I would not eat at home because there was no food in the house. My father was a fisherman; he would send us fish and food, and my mother would give the fish to her boyfriend. I would go to the neighbors' homes and sweep their yards to get food and sometimes money; my mother would stay in bed all day with her boyfriend.

My mother found out I told her boyfriend's wife he stays by the house sometimes, and she put me on the floor to sleep while my sisters slept on the bed. One night, there was a storm. It was raining and thundering real hard; my sister, Esther, told me to come in the bed, so I did. My mother then came with a bottle lamp and soaked me with kerosene oil. She then held fire over me. My sister, Esther, screamed and told my mother she was the one who told me to get in the bed. My two sisters, Joyce and Johana, wrestled with my mother to take the lamp from her. My sister Esther was screaming; it took a while to calm her down. I was afraid to sleep that night. My mother asked me why I had to talk her business.

The next morning, I went to the neighbor's, Mrs. Leila Reid's, house. They smelled the kerosene oil on me, and they called the police. When the police came, I stayed quiet because I didn't want my mother to go to prison.

My friend, Colleen Reid, cried every time she saw me. She would give me food, clothes, and money. She asked her mother to let me stay at her house, her mother told her I can only stay until six o'clock because I was a minor, and she could get in trouble, but I can always come by in the day time. Collen treated me like a sister. I was so happy for the way she treated me. Colleen ended up leaving for England with her two daughters to join her husband. She asked me to take care of her mother.

I was lost, I really missed her. I went by my friend, Violet, who also treated me well; she gave me food and clothes. I would babysit Violet's daughter, Debra, who was twelve years old at the time. My sisters, Joyce and Johana, took me to see my father; I was so happy to see him. My sisters told me not to tell my father my mother had a boyfriend at the house. My father gave me candies and ice cream; I told my father there was a man in the bed. My sisters were mad at me; they never took me back to see my father.

At fifteen years old, my mother asked me to leave the house and go live with my father. She put a few clothes in a box and put them outside the house; I didn't pick up the box. The neighbors were so mad at my mother. I went to Violet's house since she lived on the same street and spent a few months there. I then went to see my father. I told him what had happened, he sent me to his aunt, Mrs. Sarah Overton, in Carrington's Village. She took me in her house to live.

While living with my aunt, I met my first boyfriend, Gordon White, who I had my first child, Theresa, with. The relationship lasted a few years. I got a job at Plecain restaurant as a waitress. There I met my boyfriend, Mervin King; he was ten years older than I was. He was involved with me; he gave me lots of money. He would buy me four pairs of shoes, six dresses, and bags. He would shower me with gifts. I would go to his house; he never wanted me to go home so I can comb my daughter's hair. He was obsessed with me. I told him I am finished with the relationship, and he didn't want to accept it. He followed me to work. I called the police on him, and he would cry and tell the police how much he loves me. One day, I went to work, and he came in the restaurant and threw two big rocks at me and ran, causing the entire guest party to leave, which led to me getting fired immediately. One evening, while standing at the bus stop, he came and snatched my wig off my head in efforts to embarrass me, so I called my friend, Alson Ferguson, because Mervin was scared of him. A few years later, Mervin migrated to the United States where he asked me to join him, and I told him no.

A few years later, I started working at Surf Side restaurant in St. James. There I met Tennyson Harris, and then I had my second daughter, Nicole. Tennyson was a receptionist at Coral Reef Hotel. We moved in together for a few years. One day, he went to work, and I had washed his white shirts, but the clothesline in the yard was broken. A guy was passing by, and I asked him to help me with the clothesline. One of Tennyson's friends saw the guy go in the house and called Tennyson at work. I was cooking soup when Tennyson came home and was surprised when he told me I had a man in the house. I told him I asked the guy to help me put up the line in the yard so I was able to hang his clothes. He then took the pot of soup and attempted to throw it at me. I took the broom to knock the soup out of his hand, but instead, it went in his eye and broke an artery; he was hospitalized for a few weeks. I was afraid that I would go to prison; my father and his aunt sent me to Canada to Mrs. Islene Sargent for a few weeks. I got a job as a babysitter and went on my own. That was where I met Basil Lynch. He was abusive, physically and mentally. He would steal my money, and at that time, I was not a permanent resident, so he took advantage of me.

One night, he came to my apartment. He wanted money, but I did not give it to him so he cut my hands and face. My girlfriend Rosita Burman lent me her Medicare care so I can see the doctor. When they called Rosita's name, I just sat there. Rosita had to push me to go see the doctor.

I moved into another apartment thinking I could escape from Basil, but he found me one Saturday night after a party, when he started to beat me and demand sex. I ran out the apartment naked, with a towel wrapped around me, in the snow with a temperature of negative twenty-eight degrees. I got into a taxi without money. At the first stop light, I saw Sawlen Stout. I got out the taxi and went into his car and asked him to take me to Malcom Burman's house. Malcom gave me pants and slippers and called his wife, Rosita. She could not believe how I ran out the apartment.

A few months later, I moved to a new apartment where Basil found me again. I decided to marry him so I can get my residence in Canada. I went back to Barbados to collect my visa a few months after I took my daughters, Nicole and Theresa, to Canada and stayed at Basil apartment. When I went, he had a girl at the house, but he told me I can't stay in his bedroom because him and the girl would normally stay at his sister's house. A few months later, he told me I had to find somewhere to live. I found an apartment at 4270 Linton, but then Basil would show up everywhere I went.

June 1980, I was walking, and he snatched my bag with my lotto tickets and money. I called the police and made a report from 4782 Grosvenor, Queen Mary. That night, I found out that my two tickets that was stolen from me, numbers 3434 and 1978, won five hundred thousand dollars. Luckily, I wrote my daughters' names and also mine on the back of the tickets including my address. I called my husband and told him the tickets he stole from me were the winning numbers. He called me and asked me to come to his house so we can cash both tickets, but instead he would have sex with me, beat me, and ask me to leave his house. I would go home daily with a black eye, crying, which went on for months. My girlfriend, Marica Loyed, told me not to go back to his house because he had no intentions of handing over the tickets, and if I should ever go back to his house, do not call on her for help. Did I listen? No. I still went back to see him at his request and the same thing happened repetitively. His friend, Neville Morris, would always come to his house and see me in tears.

My children were hungry; we slept on cardboard boxes on the floor in an empty apartment. A few weeks later, he called me to come to his house so he can take me to cash the tickets. I took twenty dollars from his pocket so my children could get food. The next day, he called me to cash the tickets because he needed money, and he beat me so bad, my face was swollen; it took days for my face to go down.

One day, a lady from the government called my house and told me she was coming to take my children, I was so nervous, screaming and crying. I called my daughters, who were at the side of the house playing, and told them the government was going to take them away from me. My daughter, Nicole, told me to go and wash my face and to face the world; I washed my face, locked the door and went outside.

When the three government officials came to the house, they asked my daughters if there were hungry or mistreated; my daughters said no. They then left. My daughters hugged me and I broke down in tears. My daughter said, "Everything is going to be all right." I was very fortunate because if I had let them in the house, they would've seen I had no bed and was sleeping on the floor. From sleeping on the floor, we got swollen faces. My daughters would go to school without lunch, no dinner. They would tell me their belly was burning. I was on public assistance, but that was to pay rent and nothing for food. I called my husband to see if he would give me the tickets, and he would tell my friends I was crazy because if the tickets had won, he would have cashed them.

I loaned a bedroom set from a friend thinking that I would get the money when we cashed the tickets. One night, I was asleep and I heard a loud bang on my door. I called the police because there were five men with my janitor outside of my door. The police asked if I knew the janitor, and I told them yes. It was after ten o'clock; I asked the janitor why he was at my house so late. He was so mad, he didn't answer the question I asked. The next day, I went out while my daughters were at school. When I returned home, the locks for my house were changed, and my bedroom set was at the side of the building with all my clothes in garbage bags. I asked the janitor why my belongings were at the side of the building after I paid my rent, and he told me he doesn't want to lift up dead bodies. The janitor told me the men with him last night were hitmen that my husband hired, and they made him bring them to my apartment so they can kill me and dump me in the river, so they wanted me out their apartment. *My* life was in danger, and I knew they wouldn't stop until I was dead.

That evening, I cried and went to a motel on John Tolong with my daughters. At twelve o' clock, I heard a bang on my door and asked who it was, and he said, "Detective Roy from the police station."

I was familiar with the police since he was the one who took my report when I reported my husband after he snatched my bag. I opened the door and he told me to leave now because they were going to burn down the motel.

I told him, "I have nowhere to go."

He then took me and my daughters in his car to a shelter in Hennery Barasa. He asked the owner, which was a woman, to let me stay there for a few days. The owner didn't want me to stay because she was scared they would try to burn the shelter down. I stayed there for four days then she asked me to leave.

I got an apartment at 4891 Vezina; my husband found me again. I was able to get a bed and stop sleeping on the floor. My daughters started going to school again. Things started getting a bit better.

May 1981, things went bad; money was short and not much left after rent. I had to take days cleaning at Mr. Charlotte Freedman. One day, I had two quarters that was supposed to buy three French roll bread for my daughter's lunch. I dropped a quarter on the floor and went down on my knees looking for it like it was a million dollars. Four years after, my daughter, Nicole, told me she found the quarter and used it to buy candies.

June 1981, I asked a social worker, Mrs. Evelyn Fin, for her assistance. She called the head of the lotto office in Toronto and speak to a representative named Mrs. Halfway. She told Mrs. Fin the tickets were cashed by a lawyer, Albert Gomberg, and my twin sister, Dorothy Allen. She told Mrs. Fin to call her the next day; it was after four o'clock. I found that strange because to my knowledge, I did not have a twin sister. The next day, I went to Mrs. Fin's office on Van Hore where she told me my identical twin sister and her best friend, Joan Armstrong, was in her office earlier that day. She then showed me *The Journal De Moral* newspaper with my picture—that picture I gave to my sister, Joyce; she told me she was making a family album. The article stated that I was a prostitute and can't be trusted. When

I told Mrs. Fin wasn't a prostitute, and I don't have a twin sister; she called me a liar, yelled at me, and asked me to leave her office. I left in tears because she was such a good social worker who always had my best interest at heart.

A few days later, Mrs. Fin was found murdered. It was a complete shock and a memory that has stayed with me to this day. As time went by, the situation got more bizarre. I called the head office of the lotto in Toronto and spoke with Mrs. Halfway. She told me Doris Cater had died the seventh of April at the Montreal General Hospital, and she can show me the death certificate the doctor from the hospital signed. My twin sister, Dorothy Allen, head of records of the United States, and her lawyer, Albert Gomberg, took the five hundred thousand dollars in trust for my two daughters, Nicole and Theresa Carter. I was completely flabbergasted. We argued for a full five minutes over my existence. Mrs. Halfway then asked me for my social security number which I gave to her. She said, "Oh my god," and sent me to see Mr. David Clarke at the Montreal Lotto office.

July 3, 1981, I went to see Mr. Clarke, but he was unavailable, so I saw Margaret La Pierre. She told me something that I have heard in the past regarding the lotto tickets. One of the staff members, Mrs. Lynda Murray, received fifty thousand dollars from the money. She pled for me not to go to the press for the fear the government would close down the lotto office. She assured me the five hundred thousand will be paid to me and all parties involved will be prosecuted. She told me to give her four days. When I called her back, Ms. Margaret told me to come in with a lawyer; but no lawyer wanted to take the case because Mr. Gomberg was a top lawyer. I gave Mrs. Halfway a phone call to find out what was happening and she yelled at me for not waiting for Mr. David Clarke. She then told me she had seized twenty thousand dollars from Mr. Mikey Phillips who lived in Montreal. She told me Ms. Margaret La Pierre played the race card and called me a poor black woman. She then proceed to tell me the five hundred thousand was deposited into Royal Bank Van Horne and Decarie. My twin sister, Dorothy, got to keep forty thousand dollars and the rest of the money was seized by the criminal court in Montreal. All participants that were involved in the scam were tried and convicted and sentenced to six months in federal prison; they spent a few months in prison and were then pardoned. The evidence was destroyed by the court.

I went to New York for Labor Day weekend and stayed at my sister Joyce's apartment. Her best friend Esmie Albanby whispered to me that my sister does armed robberies in police uniforms. The police from 515 North Avenue Police Station in New Rochelle. I did not believe her and told my sister what Esmie told me; they were best friends in Barbados. The next month, I came back to New York to spend the weekend and asked my sister Joyce where Esmie was and she told me Esmie had been murdered. It was a complete shock and a memory that lives with me until now. Esmie was a family friend. My sister used to live with her when she ran away from home in Barbados.

I moved to New York and was living at 808 Macon Street in Brooklyn. My friend, Donna Asgil, asked me to lend her five hundred dollars to send to her daughter in Barbados. I had won four thousand dollars on the lotto win four. She came to my apartment December 18, 1993, in New York City; I told her I was going to Western Union to send money for my daughters. When she came at four o'clock, I was dressed and ready to go. She asked me to use the bathroom because she had diarrhea. We went back upstairs, and five minutes later the doorbell rang. Donna came out the bathroom because she heard the doorbell; I told her I wasn't expecting anyone. At the door, there were two women dressed in police uniforms, one of them was my twin sister who I never met. They told me they had a search warrant for my ex-boyfriend Phillip; I told them he does not live there he left one year ago. They read my rights and told me I was going to be arrested if I didn't let them in the apartment. I begged them not to arrest me. They were talking in their radios; the badge number was 317, and I let them in the apartment. My sister took my gold necklace off my neck and the jewelry from my bedroom drawer and four thousand dollars that only Donna and I knew about that was under my carpet. The telephone rang, and it was my friend, Anita Newton; I was going to take her son to Canada. When I got up to answer the phone, they held their guns to my head and told me not to move. I peed on myself, because I was scared they would kill me. Donna was still there, and they took nothing from her. They left, and Donna took me to the Eighty-First Precinct where I made a police report with a detective, where I told them I was set up by a friend because they didn't take her jewelry.

The next day, the landlord, Ms. Rita Gilford, came for the rent. I told her I didn't have it because I was robbed by two women dressed in police uniforms. She told me my friend and two women were at my apartment early in the morning, and they asked her if I was home. She said she asked them how she would know. She said she found it strange. She saw the two women dressed in police uniforms coming from the apartment; she asked them to identify themselves, and they did not. Ms. Gilford was a police sergeant at the Eighty-First Precinct; she said she took the license plate number and ran a check and found out they weren't police officers. They were arrested going through the Lincoln Tunnel, and was locked up at the 500 Port Authority Station.

My landlord, Ms. Gilford, told me to call the port authority police station to get my belongings back, but I didn't get them back. I spoke to the manager at the port authority, Mr. Mark Schaff. I then went to see him January 1994 where he sent a van to pick me up, and in his office, I met with three detectives. Mr. Gorge Nohn, who was the head detective told me it was my sisters that robbed me. I didn't believe him and we looked at footages and it was my sister, Dorothy, and her work colleague, Mrs. Blackmen—who is now head of records of the United States—dressed in police uniform, and my husband, Steve Bowen who was dressed in the sergeant uniform. Badge number 317 was driving in a white jeep coming through the Lincoln Tunnel with a lot of guns, badges, radios, nightsticks, and belts the day they robbed me, but I did not see my husband, Steven Bowen. I met him five years after I took a patient, Mrs. Eva Usdan, to Sound Shore Hospital in New Rochelle. She was there for a week. Steven was a worker at the hospital.

We left Mr. Schaff's office with the three detectives. They took me to 500 Port Authority police station where I made a police report; we then went to a lineup where there were five men and women.

There was a Spanish girl; she was crying, and they raped her behind the glass. I tried to calm down the Spanish girl, but she was devastated. On one side, there were men and the other side were women. I picked out my twin sister, Dorothy, then I saw my sister, Joyce. I couldn't believe it. I then asked the detective to go back to verify it was my sister Joyce. He told me, "No. Keep walking."

Then I saw my sister who was put in a basket at birth; I took her for my sister, Esther, who lived in Barbados. I asked the detective once more if I can check to see if it was my sister Joyce, but he turned his head and said, "I knew these were your sisters."

I told him my sister Joyce was a schoolteacher that I look up to. She was also a part of a church choir, and she's a quiet person, so it's very hard to believe. The robberies were going on for years, from 1979. They robbed a lot of people. They were arrested without appearing before the court. It was on the news channels 2, 4, and 5 daily, with headlines saying, "ROBBERY COMMITTED IN POLICE UNIFORMS."

I cried and called Mr. Schaff; he would tell me to go to the authorities. He then referred me to detective Flemmings. He also gave me a number to call, when I spoke with him on the phone. He told me those were my sisters; I should just forget about what happened. I called back Mr. Schaff, crying. He told me to go to the authorities, but no one did anything. I even called 311 for advice.

I went to Barbados for a week to see my friend, Violet; she was the one who took me in when my mother put me out her house. Violet told me my sisters do armed robberies in New York, and Joyce was locked up in New York for armed robbery, in the presence of her two children Debra and Tiny. When Violet told me that my sisters do armed robbery, her daughter Debra laughed and asked her if she was employed by CNN, because she knew details of the incident that happened with my sisters. I told Violet I was going to see my sister, Esther, who lived on the same street, and she told me not to go there because they don't like me, but I still went.

When I went to Esther, she told me Joyce was locked up in New York, and she's in a gang. I told Esther, "Violet just told me Joyce was locked up, but I didn't believe."

She then told me it was true; I sat in disbelief. I left the house and went to the supermarket and saw my mother with no shoes and her dress was dirty. They held her for food she stole from the store, so I paid for it. I then told my mother I paid for the food, and she stormed off. I went looking for her but couldn't find her. I called Esther and told her what happened. Esther started to tell me our mother left home; I couldn't believe they had her walking the streets looking like that.

February 2003, my sister Joyce called me and told me our brother, Carlyle, was very sick and she wanted me to go and see him. She gave me his phone number; I called him and went to his house in Queens with my husband. I brought him soup and told him Joyce told me to come and help him. I told him to let Joyce come to help since she lived close by, but he told me, in the presence of his wife and my husband, that Joyce does armed robbery in police uniform in the city, and he wants nothing to do with her. I was shock when he told me, but I didn't say anything. I asked if he needed money, and he told me he had eighty thousand dollars in the bank because he had a fishing boat in Barbados that markets a lot of money, and had to take the boat from our brother, Joey, since he wasn't getting any money from him. He gave it to his friend to supervise. They would go out for two weeks and give him money. I asked my brother's wife if my sister Joyce can come help her and she said no because she is on drugs. I was so ashamed. I told my brother I was leaving, and he told me he had something to tell me when he comes back. He went to Barbados for a week.

That day, when I got home, my sister Joyce called me to find out what my brother told me, and I told her nothing. She wanted to know if my brother had money, but I didn't let her know my brother and I spoke about his money.

March 2003, Carlyle died. I went to the funeral and saw my sisters. I was with my husband and two daughters. I saw Esther and touched her while saying hi. She then elbowed me. I thought it was strange because we didn't have any problems. Half hour later, Esther came and said hello; she was wearing a white top and a black skirt. I told her I touched someone earlier thinking it was her, and the woman elbowed me and said nothing. I told Esther that the woman was her twin sister that was born first, and when she was born, the midwife placed her in a basket on a table. I told her about the incident when the midwife cut her on the top lip and took her sister and left.

I was looking for my husband at the funeral and couldn't find him. He was out in the car with my twin sister, Dorothy. She was pregnant at the time for my husband, Steven. I didn't know she gave birth to a baby boy in 2003. When I saw him, I asked who he was talking to, and he replied, "To a friend." I was upset and didn't want to go to the repast because I didn't want to be around my family.

April 28, 2003, I wrote a letter to the mayor regarding the lack of service I received when I visited city hall at 515 North Avenue. I went to the office to obtain a copy of my marriage certificate where I met my twin sister, Dorothy. I was in line waiting to sign and was surprised to see her. I told the guy that was standing behind me that my sister robbed me. He laughed and told me she's head of records of the United States and she looks like me. When I went to sign my name, she told the officer to scratch my name out the book; he was looking at me and her. I filled out the form for a copy of my marriage certificate, and she told the clerk there's no records here on file for Doris Carter Bowen or Steven Bowen, and that was the first time I saw my sister since she robbed me at gunpoint on December 18, 1993, in New York City.

I didn't get a reply from the mayor of New Rochelle. I got a marriage certificate my sister, Dorothy, made out that was no good. I went back a few weeks later and got another marriage certificate that was no good again; it didn't have a seal or stamp—it was just a piece of paper with my name and my husband's name, and I paid fifteen dollars for the form.

In 2003, I asked my husband to leave my apartment in Brooklyn, which he did while I was at work. My sister, Dorothy, took my jewelry and money, and I made a police report to the Eighty-First Precinct and then asked Mrs. Betsy Gotham, a public advocate for the city of New York, to write a letter to deputy inspector Robert Bowen NYPD Eighty-First Precinct, 30 Ralph Avenue, about the robberies that took place at my apartment. Deputy Inspector Robert Bowen retired in 2004. My cousin Joan Roche's husband got shot on the street, and she asked me to keep the repast at my apartment; we went to the store to buy foil pans and two guys that were standing outside the store told me that I was a police officer that took their money, drugs, and jewelry. I told them am not police, and they called me a liar, then my cousin told me they had mistaken me for my sister, Dorothy. I was scared to go back to the store which was three doors down from my apartment. I got two of my friends, Joel Bailey and Keith Tull, to walk me to my apartment each time I would go to the corner store. The guys moved from standing in front the store for years; people thought I was a police officer. Until this day a guy from Jamaica thinks am a police officer; he thinks I am my sister.

In 2004, my cousin, Annie Carter, was arrested and charged for a murder of a bank manager he pulled over in his SUV with a city police badge, They had a press conference at Grand Central Station with the mayor and governor and the police chief; my cousin was a manager at Altman's store years ago. I was scared for my safety.

June 2005, I went to the district of police office in Brooklyn and asked them to please take my sisters off the streets and a gang of postal workers, bank tellers, INS Immigration Officers. The district attorney gave them weekends of community service, from July 2005 to July 2006, which didn't help because they went back doing armed robberies again in 2007.

I went to take Mrs. Hazel Demarchais to Irvington Senior Center where I met the best friend of my sister Dorothy, Joan Armstrong, who was the director of the center. I went to the senior center three times weekly and found out in 2009 that she was the Joan Armstrong that was arrested in Canada and locked up in federal prison and also at Port Authority Police station, where she was in the lineup with my twin sister.

June 2009, my twin sister, Dorothy, passed away, and I would talk to Joan not knowing she wanted to have me arrested after my sister died at the Senior center. She told me she would help me to recover the money that was seized by the courts in Montreal, Canada.

She asked me to take Mrs. Hazel home and come back, and I told her I can't leave her alone, but she can come to the house.

February 2, 2010, she called me at eleven o'clock and told me she was coming. At 11:15, she rang the doorbell and asked me to come outside. I told her I can't leave my patient alone in the house, so she came in and sat at the bottom of the step. She took my picture with her cellphone. I asked her why she took the picture but she never answered. I told her if she wanted to help me, she has to come clean regarding her being arrested and being in federal prison and if she committed the murder of social worker Mrs. Finn. She left and told me she will be back.

At 12:30, the doorbell rang. It was two detectives dressed in white T-shirts and black pants. One of the men was Joan's son who was a police officer. They told me they had a complaint from Joan that I harassed her. I asked, "How can I harass her when she came to see me at my house?" I explained to the officer about me asking her if she was arrested in Canada and a murder that took place in Canada and she got up and left. Her son went up the stairs and back down and asked me for my ID then left.

At 6:12, the doorbell rang; it was the sergeant that was there earlier, dressed in police uniform. He told me to sign a letter, and that if I didn't sign the letter, I would've been arrested. I was restricted from going to Irvington Senior Center premises and couldn't attend any functions. I was so nervous I couldn't sign my name. I told them I have been going to the Senior Center for two years and never had a problem with anyone there. I told him Joan was the reason he was doing this to me, and he left.

I called Mrs. Demarchais' son, Ranal, and told him what the sergeant had me sign and the restrictions. He thought it was strange. I then told him I was leaving the job, and he would have to find someone else to stay there. It was a very bad experience from the police department of Irvington because I was banded from the center and the stores in the area.

October 4, 2013, I hired a lawyer, Gabrielle Marcus, who was referred by the Canadian Embassy in New York. I gave him one hundred and seventy-five dollars for consultation and two thousand in cashier's checks, and I didn't hear from him until two years later. When I called him, he said he was going to Canada for the weekend and he will get back to me. Each time I called, he was in Canada in court. Then I went to the Canadian embassy and made a complaint. I then put a note in his mail box and demanded him to call me back. He told me he was looking about my case in Canada, and he would call me when he gets back. He left a message on my phone saying he had good news from the courts in Canada, and we'd discuss it when he got back.

On his return, he called and informed me he didn't find anything in the courts in Canada. I then remind him of the voicemail. He told me to give him two weeks and he would get back to me, but he never did. He found out I wrote a letter of complaint to Anderson Cooper of CNN. A few days later, he called and asked if he could speak with me. I found out he was lying to me about the case in Canada. When he called, I told him he was a liar, and I would report him to the bar association. He came to my job banging on the front door wanting to speak with me, but I called the police. He told the police he was overseen the five thousand in escrow, then he told the bar association I was crazy and asked my daughter to take me to see the doctor. I was never crazy. I contacted the federal agent in Canada who sent me to the Clarkston police station where I spoke to the sergeant to make a report for the federal agent 9944 from the RCMP. He did not want to speak with the agent 9944; he wanted to speak with someone with a name. So I called the federal agent 9944 and gave him the phone. I was at the window then he called me inside. He told the agent on the phone he was speaking to Mrs. Doris Carter who has dual citizenship. They wanted to pick up Mr. Marcus. I told the federal agent 9944 I wanted to get the money and have him arrested. I then told the federal agent that am going to the attorney grievance committee, and he told me they can't make lawyer Marcus give me any money, because the crime was committed in Canada not America. When I hired lawyer Marcus, he told me he had jurisdiction in Canada and America. I wrote a letter to the courts in Montreal for documentations for the case that went to the courts on July 1981 for Albert Gomberg, five hundred thousand dollars on the system. I wrote a letter to the archives; the receptionist Mrs. Helen Chartrand changed the date to 1983, then I called back the courts and spoke to Mr. Lucbeaudet and told him that Mrs. Chartrand had changed the date to 1983. He gave me the docket number 500-27-032-122-832 and sent me the court document profile. The evidence was destroyed, and the parties that went to federal prison were pardoned by the court. I found out from the judge that only my two daughters can claim the money in Canada. They claimed I had died the seventh of April and put money in trust funds of my daughters, Nicole and Theresa Carter. Lawyer Albert Gomberg, my twin sister, Dorothy, my ex-sister-in-law Angela Smith issued a death certificate to the lotto office to cash the two lotto tickets, and the doctor from the Montreal General Hospital signed the death certificate. The money that was seized by the courts in 1981 was put into an escrow for four hundred, and fifty-five thousand was recovered; my sister, Dorothy, got to keep forty thousand dollars. My ex-sister-in-law Angela Smith was charged for traffic ticket in ossin. She got charged for money, that's how they cover it up in the courts. My ex, estranged husband, Basil Lynch was in the courts for alimony, five hundred thousand dollars.

On the ninth April 2010 at 2:45 p.m., I receive a call from Mrs. Lynda Murray from the lotto office in Montreal, Quebec, Canada. She told me a lawyer came to the office on my behalf to claim $500,000 that was in escrow. At the time, I was on the train, so I told her I would call her back Monday morning. She then gave me her extension (2297).

I called her Monday morning at 9:25 a.m. I thought something was wrong because she spoke with a West Indian accent on Friday and a French accent on Monday. She told me she knew that I didn't send any lawyer on my behalf. She told me she was working on my behalf, and in three days, a prosecutor will be calling me. He will go to the courts to get the money out of escrow. I will finally receive the money afterwards on the thirteenth April at 8:55 a.m.

When I called Mrs. Murray, something struck me as strange because now she spoke with a Barbadian accent. When I confronted her about her accents, she just told me she was the one I spoke to on Friday. At this point, I believed this was all a prank. She then proceeded to tell me that she forwarded the case to the prosecutors, and I will be receiving the money in three days. I called back in four days to inform her that I didn't hear from the prosecutor. She assured me he would call on the twenty-first of April.

I received a call from the prosecutor, Mr. Mike Duranceau. He told me he was now receiving the case. He asked me for the tickets' numbers and any letters I received from the lotto. I thought that was strange because Mrs. Murray told me she forwarded my case with all the information to him. He gave me his telephone number (514-499-7111 Ext. 3425), fax number 873-3423, and said he will call me in a few days when the money was out of escrow. I waited a full week and didn't receive a call. I called Mr. Duranceau but got no answer for the next two days. I called repeatedly, but once again, got no response. I called Mrs. Murray to complain and threatened to come to Canada with my lawyer as soon as possible on the fifth May at four p.m.

Mr. Duranceau finally called. He told me he was away for the last ten days. He also told me to call him only after I called back the lotto office and spoke to Ms. Natalie Wester. She told me she knew all about my case and forwarded my call to Mr. Duranceau. He told me he was very busy with fifty other cases besides mine, and he will get back to me in a few days. I haven't heard from him since.

My twin sister, Dorothy was horrible. She lived a double life: she was on drugs and robbed people in police uniforms and got away with all the crimes she committed. She ran a gang in New York, and sat down next to the mayor of New Rochelle City Hall. When the mayor found out her crimes, he resigned for personal reasons; she got arrested without appearing in front of a judge since she was head of records for United States. These robberies and murders went on for years, and now her daughter took over the gang. She is currently an engineer at Con Edison. I'm ashamed of my sisters and their lifestyle.

I was trying to get this money, and all I got was run around; now they're saying I'm crazy.

I want this book to be published so the truth can be revealed.

Thank you in advance, Doris Carter.

Doris Carter

About the Author

Doris Carter is a woman of strong faith and virtue. She is a selfless, caring human being who would give anyone her last. She is strong-willed, resilient, and persistent, as she always seeks to be the best that she can be. She is ambitious and determined as she never gives up on her dreams despite overcoming some tough circumstances.

Doris wishes to thank you for taking this journey with her. She has never in her life thought that her family and so-called friends would put her through all this because she would give the shirt off her back if someone needed it. She is ashamed of her sisters and their lifestyle choices. All she wanted to do was get her money, and all she got was the run around; now they're all saying she's crazy! She wants this book to be published so the truth can be revealed.

CPSIA information can be obtained
at www.ICGtesting.com
Printed in the USA
BVHW080411070721
611240BV00011B/1583